NEW BOOKS FOR NEW READERS

Judy Cheatham
*General Editor*

# Women Who Made a Difference

*Carol Crowe-Carraco*

THE UNIVERSITY PRESS OF KENTUCKY

The New Books for New Readers project was made possible through funding from the National Endowment for the Humanities, the Kentucky Humanities Council, and the Scripps-Howard Foundation. The opinions expressed in this book are not necessarily those of the Kentucky Humanities Council.

Cover illustrations (clockwise from upper left) are courtesy of: Robert Dunnigan; Loretta Lynn; Margaret I. King Library, University of Kentucky; The Filson Club; and Frontier Nursing Service.

Copyright © 1989 by the Kentucky Humanities Council

Published by The University Press of Kentucky
Scholarly publisher for the Commonwealth,
serving Bellarmine University, Berea College, Centre College of Kentucky, Eastern Kentucky University, The Filson Historical Society, Georgetown College, Kentucky Historical Society, Kentucky State University,
Morehead State University, Murray State University, Northern Kentucky University, Transylvania University, University of Kentucky, University of Louisville, and Western Kentucky University.
All rights reserved.

Editorial and Sales Offices: The University Press of Kentucky
663 South Limestone Street, Lexington, Kentucky 40508-4008
www.kentuckypress.com

09 08 07 06 05          8 7 6 5 4

Library of Congress Cataloging-in-Publication Data

Crowe-Carraco, Carol, 1943–
    Women who made a difference / Carol Crowe-Carraco.
        p.          cm.—(New books for new readers)
    ISBN 0-8131-0901-9
    1. Women—Kentucky—Biography. 2. Readers for new literates.
I. Title. II. Series.
HQ1438.K4C76      1989
305.4'092'2—dc20                              89-38085
[B]
ISBN 978-0-8131-0901-5

This book is printed on acid-free recycled paper meeting the requirements of the American National Standard for Permanence in Paper for Printed Library Materials.

Manufactured in the United States of America.

Member of the Association of
American University Presses

# Contents

# Foreword

The New Books for New Readers project was made possible through funding from the National Endowment for the Humanities, the Kentucky Humanities Council, and *The Kentucky Post*. The co-sponsorship and continuing assistance of the Kentucky Department for Libraries and Archives and the Kentucky Literacy Commission have been essential to our undertaking. We are also grateful for the advice and support provided to us by the University Press of Kentucky. All these agencies share our commitment to the important role that reading books should play in the lives of the people of our state, and their belief in this project has made it possible.

The Kentucky Humanities Council recognizes in the campaign for adult literacy a cause closely linked to our own mission, to make the rich heritage of the humanities accessible to all Kentuckians. Because the printed word is a vital source of this heritage, we believe that books focused on our state's history and culture and written for adults who are newly learning to read can help us to serve a group of Kentucky's citizens not always reached or served by our programs. We offer these books in the hope that they will be of value to adult new readers in their quest, through words, for an understanding of what it means to be human.

Ramona Lumpkin, Executive Director
Kentucky Humanities Council

# Preface

Why a book about Kentucky women? There is an easy answer. Women helped shape the history of the state. Women were there for more than 200 years. Their lives are worth reading about. They have had much more effect than many people think.

A 19th-century English woman, Jane Austen, once wrote, "History tells me nothing that does not either vex or weary me. The quarrels of popes and kings, with wars . . . on every page. The men all so good for nothing and hardly any women at all. It is very tiresome."

The same has been true in Kentucky history. Much is written about males and little about females. Women should not be lost from history. Their lives are very interesting, too.

More women should be included in this book. But choices had to be made. I hope my choices will do two things. First, these nine women will interest readers. Second, these nine stories will make readers want to learn about other women who made a difference in Kentucky's history.

Writers always owe debts when they are writing. I want to thank the following members of the Barren County Literacy Program for helping me: J.B. Arms, Billy Duvall, Sr., Linda Goad, Eva Neal, and Margie Patton. Thanks also go to Nancy Baird and Lowell Harrison for being the first readers of this book. And, of course, my thanks to my family. Bob, Sarah Beth, and Will—the kitchen table is no longer my desk!

Carol Crowe-Carraco

For Sarah E. D. Carraco
Sara C. Marcum
Martha M. Simonton
Marie C. Supplee

# Jenny Wiley, 1760–1831: Pioneer

Most stories about Pioneer Kentucky tell very little about pioneer women. Females are usually seen as weak and scared. Yet women shared the same hardships as men. They had to be just as brave to live in a new land. Jenny Wiley was one of these strong, brave women.

Virginia (Jenny) Sellards was born in Pennsylvania in 1760. When she was three, the Sellards moved to western Virginia near the Kentucky frontier. They built a log cabin on Walker's Creek.

The Sellards were not educated people. But they wanted a better life for their four children. Jenny's mother taught her children to work hard. She always said, "Keep clean and be brave."

Jenny's father loved his land, but he hated the Indians. He never admitted that the Native Americans had any right to the land. He warned, "Watch and listen for Indians. Kill them before they kill us."

Jenny never went to school. She could only read and write her name. She liked to spin and weave. She also worked in the fields and was a sure shot with a gun. Jenny knew the dangers of the frontier. She was not afraid of the hardships of pioneer life.

In 1778 Jenny married Thomas Wiley. Thomas had just come from Ireland. He knew nothing about being a pioneer. Thomas often depended on Jenny's frontier skills.

Jenny and Thomas Wiley built their own log cabin and cleared the land. They planted corn, wheat, and flax. They had horses, mules, sheep, cows, chickens, and dogs. In time they also had three sons and a daughter.

The Wileys were happy in their valley. But some of their friends were not. Tice Harman and others wanted to move on west. In September 1789, Harman led a group of hunters to Kentucky. They camped on John's Creek.

The Indians did not want the white men in their hunting ground. A small band of about 20 Shawnee and Cherokee attacked the Harman party. Several of the warriors were killed.

To get even, the Indians attacked cabins in Virginia. They planned to burn the Harman homestead. But they did not know where it was. They struck the Wileys' cabin by mistake.

Thomas was away from home. Jenny, her children, and her brother fought for their very lives. But it did no good. The Indians killed and scalped the Sellard boy and three of the Wiley children. They did not kill pregnant Jenny Wiley or her son Tom, who was 15 months old. The Indians took Jenny and Tom with them to Kentucky.

For four days Jenny Wiley kept up with the Indians. When she and the baby fell behind, one of the braves grabbed Tom. The Indian held the little boy's feet and bashed his head against a tree. Then he scalped Tom as Jenny watched.

They left the dead boy where he fell. The party marched on north to their winter camp. During the winter Jenny Wiley gave birth to a baby boy. She named him Robert Bruce for a Scottish hero.

Mother and baby survived the winter. But little Bobby failed an Indian test of manhood in the spring. The braves tied the baby to a piece of bark and floated him in the creek. When the baby cried in fear, they killed him. Jenny saw him die, also.

In a few weeks the Indians moved to a salt lick on Little Mud Creek. Jenny Wiley had to do all the jobs of the camp. She gutted and skinned the animals the Indians killed. She tanned hides, planted corn, gathered wood, and did the cooking. She carried ore from a nearby lead mine and made bullets.

The Indians treated Jenny just the way they treated all women. They expected women to cook, tan hides, plant corn, gather firewood, and make bullets. Women were to fetch and carry. The Indians also gave all infant prisoners the same test they gave little Robert Bruce. In the Indian world, the weak and timid died.

In the fall of 1790 Jenny Wiley heard the warriors plan to move north of the Ohio River. She knew she must escape. Jenny left the camp while the Indians were away hunting. She walked downstream. As long as she stayed in the water, she did not leave a trail. She feared the Indians would catch up with her. The blowing wind seemed to say, "Run, Jenny, run. Hurry. Hurry. Hurry."

She became tired. She lay down to rest and fell asleep. When she awakened, she heard the footsteps of the Indians. They did not find her. The next day she followed the creek to a trail. She ran along the trail. When the trail forked, she followed the creek now named in her honor.

At dawn on the second day, Jenny saw the fort at Harman's Station on John's Creek. She called out, "Help! Help! I am Jenny Wiley." She crossed the river and joined her friends.

As winter began, Tice Harman and others took

Jenny Wiley back to Virginia. Along the way Indians attacked the group several times. Jenny joined in the battles. She took a rifle and killed several of her foes.

Back at home, Jenny became the object of much talk. People looked at her and shook their heads. Had she become an Indian woman? Had she liked her life with the Indians? Why did it take her so long to escape?

As the frontier moved westward, so did the Wileys. In the early 1800s they came to the Big Sandy Valley. They settled near where Jenny had been held captive. The Wileys built another log cabin. They cleared land and planted crops. They raised their family of five more children and taught them to live on the frontier.

Thomas Wiley died in 1810. Jenny lived until 1831. Today they are both buried on a shady hill near the town of River in Johnson County. Jenny Wiley State Park in Floyd County is named in her honor.

Jenny Wiley was a pioneer woman who faced many problems. She survived being an Indian prisoner. She survived the hardships of frontier life.

In later years Jenny Wiley became a folk heroine. The story of her life was often told by the pioneers. There is even a story that a mother could say, "Jenny Wiley," and her children would come running. To children the words had a message. They said, "Stay close or the Indians will get you."

# Lucy Audubon, 1787–1874: Nineteenth-Century Wife

Kentucky became a state in 1792. The forts and lonely cabins of pioneer days slowly gave way to small towns. Families changed the way they lived. A woman's life depended on how rich her husband and father were. Women were usually homemakers. But sometimes they had to get jobs. Lucy Audubon was such a woman.

Lucy Bakewell Audubon was born in England in 1787. The Bakewells were wealthy. Unlike most men of the day, Lucy's father thought that girls should be educated. He sent her to school. Lucy was a good student, and she liked history, geography, and science. Lucy also enjoyed music and the outdoor life. She swam, boated, and rode horses.

In the early 1800s the Bakewells moved to America. They settled in Pennsylvania on a large farm. Lucy spent her time sewing, reading, and playing the piano.

Sometimes she helped her younger brothers and sisters with their lessons. She did not concern herself with housework. She did not worry about money. Her family gave her everything she wanted.

But Lucy was very lonely. Few young people lived in the area. She longed for her own home, husband, and children. "I want to marry a great man," she said.

In 1804 Lucy met John James Audubon. He was a charming Frenchman who came to America to avoid the army. He talked and dressed like a gentleman. He was also a painter. He stated, "Someday I will paint a picture of every bird in the country."

Lucy's father felt that the Frenchman was not ready for marriage. Audubon had no serious interests. Drawing, dancing, and hunting were not ways to support a wife. But at last the Bakewells agreed to the marriage. The wedding took place in April 1808, and Lucy's family gave them $5,000 as a gift.

Lucy and John James used the money to set up a business in Louisville, Kentucky. Audubon opened a clothing store, and the couple lived at the Indian Queen Hotel. Lucy enjoyed hotel life, but she longed for her own home. Audubon spent too much time away from the store. He painted bird pictures in the woods. He bought fine horses and guns.

Audubon's store did not succeed, and in 1810 it closed. John James, Lucy, and a baby son moved to

Henderson, a town of 20 families. It needed a clothing store.

In Henderson, Lucy turned a dirty cabin into a cozy home. She used her mother's dishes and silverware. She scrubbed, cooked, and cared for the baby. Her hands were often rough and red. John James was supposed to be running the store. But he often left it and went to the woods to paint.

As Ohio River traffic grew, Audubon's business grew. Soon he borrowed money to buy land and add to the store. He built mills to cut logs and grind corn into meal.

The Audubons also bought a larger home. Lucy laid out a garden and planted fruit trees. She filled the house with cherry and walnut furniture and hired servants. They had a library of 150 books. The Henderson house began to look like Lucy's childhood homes.

Lucy Audubon enjoyed life in Henderson. She had two more children. She attended turkey shoots, horse races, and weddings. She often had guests in her home. Lucy Audubon was very happy. She said, "I love my life as a wife and mother."

But during the 1819 depression money grew scarce. Store accounts were hard to collect. The mills had very little business. When bills came due, Audubon began to sell property. He sold land and then the house and furniture. Finally he sold Lucy's china and silverware.

Lucy now faced the scorn of Henderson. She said, "People say things that hurt. Friendship goes when poverty comes." Things grew worse. John James was arrested in Louisville and put in jail for debt. Lucy packed the family's belongings and went to him. Arriving in Louisville, she learned that her husband was out of jail. Audubon had admitted he had no money and declared bankruptcy. He also stated, "I am rich because I have Lucy."

Lucy Audubon was an unhappy woman. She was ashamed of her family's problems. Two of their children died during this period, also. Lucy said, "Only a woman can know the pain I feel." She was broken-hearted. But she became the family's only support.

Few good jobs were open to women. Teaching, however, was an acceptable job. Lucy became a teacher. She said, "If I can keep children on a subject for five minutes, they will never forget what I teach them."

John James Audubon went to New Orleans. He hoped to paint pictures of people while he finished his study of American birds. Lucy and their two sons joined him in Louisiana. She found work again as a teacher. Lucy grew bitter under the strain, but she believed that her husband would be a great man some day.

Audubon did publish his pictures. *Birds of America* came out in four books between 1827 and 1838. They sold for $4,000. ($4,000 for four books was a great deal of money then. Most people worked for less than a dollar a day.)

Lucy was pleased. She enjoyed the next 20 years. The Audubons traveled to England and Scotland. They settled in New York on a large farm.

John James Audubon's death in 1851 ended Lucy's happiness. Soon their son's bad planning wiped out the family's money. In 1858, at the age of 71, Lucy again took a job as a teacher. She taught school for the next ten years.

In the late 1860s, Lucy Audubon lost her eyesight and quit teaching. She went back to Kentucky to live with a granddaughter. She died in Shelbyville in 1874.

On her deathbed she insisted that she would not have changed a minute of her life. She had been a homemaker and a teacher. She had survived family shame and debt. She had also married a great man. John James Audubon's name and work had become an important part of United States history.

Lucy Audubon was a remarkable 19th-century woman. She had the important traits of a pioneer woman and a fine lady. She worked hard. She was loyal to her husband and loved her family. Lucy Audubon did what had to be done.

# Malinda Gatewood Bibb, c. 1815– ?: Slave

By the middle of the 19th century, Kentucky's population was nearly one million. About 11 percent of these people were slave women. These black females had no rights at all. They could be beaten by their owners. They could be sold away from their families. Those who could ran off. Most did not.

Long stories about the lives of women slaves would be very interesting. But they did not or could not write their stories down. Only brief outlines of their lives can be found. Something is known about the short life of one slave, Malinda Gatewood Bibb. Her story tells much about the sad lives of Kentucky slaves.

Malinda Gatewood Bibb lived in Bedford, Trimble County, Kentucky, in the 1830s. She was born about 1815, but her real birth date is lost. She did not know her father's name. Her mother was a free black woman. Malinda had light brown skin and dark, beautiful eyes. William Gatewood, a farmer, owned her.

When she was seventeen, Malinda fell in love with Henry Bibb. He was a slave, too. He was owned by a family in nearby Oldham County. Henry Bibb wanted to be free. He had once run away. But he had been found and brought back. He had plans to run away again. He would cross the Ohio River to the free state of Indiana. Then he would make his way north to Canada.

Malinda shared Henry's dream of freedom. They got married at Christmas in 1833. They did not have a preacher. Slave marriages were not legal in Kentucky. Malinda and Henry held hands and promised to be true to one another. They also asked God to bless their being together.

Within a few months, William Gatewood bought Henry. The Bibbs could now live together. Henry found life on the Gatewood farm to be terrible. Gatewood raped Malinda several times a week. He also cursed and beat her. Henry and Malinda could do nothing to stop such treatment.

In 1834 Malinda gave birth to a baby girl. The Bibbs named her Mary Frances. Malinda returned to the fields soon after her child's birth. She left Frances with her mistress. Mrs. Gatewood abused the little girl. She whipped and slapped her.

Malinda and Henry wanted a better life for their

family. They made their plans. Henry would run away. He would take the Underground Railroad to Canada. The Underground Railroad was a network of routes and hiding places. It helped some runaway slaves reach safety in northern states and Canada.

Henry left Kentucky in 1837. Malinda prayed every night that Henry would return for them. He tried three times to rescue them. Each time the Gatewoods learned of the plans and stopped them.

In July 1839, Henry returned again to Kentucky and was caught. William Gatewood decided to sell the three Bibbs. A slave who had run away would probably try to run away again. Gatewood also feared that Henry had told Malinda about the stops on the Underground Railroad. She might tell others, and he would lose all his slaves.

Gatewood took the Bibbs to Louisville to be sold. He housed them in a dirty jail. Both Malinda and Frances cried when the fleas bit them. "Make the bugs stop, Mama," the little girl screamed.

Madison Garrison, a slave trader, bought the Bibbs for $1,000. He would sell them "down the river" in New Orleans for a profit. The slave trader planned to use Malinda for his own pleasure. She fought him off, and he beat her. Her clothes were stained with blood, but she did not give in to him.

At the New Orleans slave market, Malinda and the

others combed their hair and washed their faces. Garrison also made them bathe in greasy dish water. He wanted their skin to look slick so they would bring a higher price.

Francis Whitfield bought the Bibb family for $1,200. Whitfield did not rape slave women. But he worked all his slaves hard and fed them little. If they became sick, he gave them homemade medicine.

Malinda became ill. She said, "I am so sick. Let me die." She did not die, but her newborn daughter did. Whitfield would not let Henry make a coffin. So Malinda and Henry buried her in the ground without one.

Soon Henry decided to run away again. This time he took Malinda and Frances with him. They spent ten days in a Louisiana swamp. They lived on wild fruit. Henry fought alligators and snakes. Malinda killed a wolf with a club. Whitfield used dogs to find them. They tried to run, but they were caught.

Whitfield whipped both Henry and Malinda. They were in great pain. In December 1840, Whitfield sold Henry to a group of gamblers. But he would not sell Malinda and Frances to them. When Malinda begged to go too, Whitfield beat her.

Malinda and Henry never saw each other again. Henry ran away from his new owners and made his way back to Canada. During the 1840s and 1850s he gave speeches about the evils of slavery. He also ran a newspaper.

Malinda Bibb and her daughter were sold once more in Louisiana. In 1845 she sent news to friends in Kentucky. She had become the mistress of her new owner. Malinda begged her friends to tell Henry what she had done. He must forgive and forget her. She had no one to help her, and she had to take care of Frances.

There is no record of Malinda Gatewood Bibb after 1845. Her thirty known years were filled with some happiness and much pain. Her story tells about the evils of slavery. She should be remembered.

# Laura Clay, 1849–1941: Suffragist

During much of the 19th century, Kentucky women had few rights. A woman could own property. But if she married, the property became her husband's. She had no legal say-so over her children. Although widows and unwed females paid taxes, women could not vote. Laura Clay worked to change these things. She was a suffragist, and she took part in many struggles to get rights for women. Suffragists wanted the vote for women. They believed if women could vote they could get other rights.

Laura Clay was born in 1849 at her family's 2,500-acre farm, White Hall, near Richmond, Kentucky. (Today White Hall is owned by the state and is open to the public.) Her mother, Mary Jane Warfield Clay, raised Laura and her five brothers and sisters. Her father, Cassius Clay, was seldom at home. He made trips to the Northeast to talk about the evils of slavery.

He also spent eight years in Russia as the American minister to that country.

Laura's mother wanted all her children to get an education. Laura attended a small school near White Hall. At the age of 14 she enrolled at Sayre Female Institute (Sayre School today) in Lexington. She took classes in foreign languages, chemistry, and history. Unlike other schools, Sayre did not have classes to prepare girls to be wives and mothers.

At Sayre, Laura became aware of her brains and ability. She kept a diary. She wrote in it, "I am a woman. I have a better mind than many boys my age." She also stated, "I know there will be women's rights someday."

Laura Clay finished Sayre in 1865. Then she had a year of school in New York. But her father saw no reason for further education for Laura, and she came home. She spent the next few years helping her mother.

In 1869 Cassius Clay returned from Russia. The stories of his many Russian girlfriends reached Kentucky before he did. Mary Jane Clay was not happy, and there were bitter fights between them. In 1870 Clay's four-year-old Russian son arrived at White Hall. Mary Jane Clay moved to Lexington.

The Clays' 45-year marriage ended in divorce in 1878. Under Kentucky law, Mrs. Clay got nothing. Her years of running White Hall and paying her husband's debts did not count. Cassius Clay said that she owed him $80,000 for rent during the years she had lived at White Hall. But he did not try to get it. Mary Jane Clay was lucky. She had money from her dead parents. Otherwise, she would have faced poverty.

Her mother's troubles had a great effect upon Laura Clay. She said, "I am not blind. I see the unfair position of women under Kentucky law. Women are not equal now. I must work to make things fair." Laura Clay never married, and she gave all her time to women's causes.

Laura's sisters were already suffragists. She joined them. The Clay women believed that God had blessed the struggle for women's rights. "Suffrage is God's cause," Laura said, "and God leads our plans."

Not all Kentucky women wanted suffrage. Some were afraid that changes would hurt them. Laura Clay stated, "It is such a pity. Women do not trust each other."

Many Kentucky newspapers made fun of Laura Clay and the suffragists. They were called "Silly Sallies" and "Crazy Janes." The newspapers stated, "Voting is a man's job. Women should stay home."

From 1888 to 1912 Laura Clay headed the Kentucky Equal Rights Association. This group got things done. They forced the Kentucky legislature to make new laws. By 1900 married women could own property and control their own money. They could also make wills.

Laws provided female doctors for the state's hospitals and prisons for women.

In 1895 Laura joined the National Woman Suffrage Association. She gave speeches across the country about suffrage. She was a large woman, and her loud voice could be heard. She loved making speeches. She said, "I am in my glory."

Laura Clay, however, thought that votes for women should come through state law. She did not approve of a voting amendment to the United States Constitution. Most of the country's suffrage leaders wanted a national amendment. They said that the national route would be quicker than getting the vote in each state.

Laura disagreed, and she resigned from the National Woman Suffrage Association. She also dropped out of the Kentucky Equal Rights Association for the same reason. She had mixed feelings when Kentucky passed the 19th Amendment in 1920. She was glad to have the vote. But she hated a national amendment to the United States Constitution.

During the 1920s Laura Clay led an active political life. She voted on state and national questions. In 1923 she ran for the Kentucky State Senate. She lost, but she was not sad. She said, "I am helping Kentucky women to take a stronger interest in their rights."

After 1930 Laura Clay made few public appearances. She did oppose a move to pay male teachers more than female teachers. She argued for "equal pay for equal work." She stated, "Children cannot be led to believe that men are better than women."

During the last years of her life, Laura Clay worked to reform the government of her church. She insisted that women should help direct the workings of the Episcopal Church. Thanks to her efforts, reforms came. Women became voting delegates to church conferences. The Episcopal Church also allowed women students to attend the University of the South in Tennessee.

Laura Clay died on June 29, 1941. She was 92 years old. She was buried in the Lexington Cemetery.

Kentucky suffragist Laura Clay helped gain the right to vote for women. She also worked for legal rights, equal pay, and education. Much progress was made, but more needed to be done. Her fight continues today.

# Enid Yandell, 1869–1934: Sculptor

Sculptors make forms in clay and stone. Many people thought that women could not be successful sculptors because they did not have the strength to work in clay and stone. But Enid Yandell knew that she could be a sculptor. She became a pioneer, just like her best known statue, "Daniel Boone."

Born just after the Civil War, Enid Yandell grew up in Louisville. Her father, who died when she was 14, was a well-known doctor. Her mother enjoyed painting. Enid liked the same things her parents did. She studied and drew the human body.

In 1887 Enid began classes at the Cincinnati Academy of Art. She learned to draw life-like pictures of the human body. Her pictures showed people with and without their clothes. Her mother warned her to tell no one about the nude pictures. "Everyone in Kentucky will be shocked," she said.

At the academy Enid began the serious study of sculpture. She copied statues of Greek gods and goddesses. In 1889 she received the school's senior prize for a statue of a Greek god.

In 1891 Enid Yandell went to Chicago to work on the sculpture for the Chicago World's Fair of 1893. She molded pieces from early in the morning until six in the evening. Her pay was five dollars a day.

Yandell's work was exciting but tiring. "My hands and arms get so tired," she declared. Many days she handled 2,000 pounds of clay. But her muscles grew strong. She said, "Sculpture builds muscles. It is better than sports for muscle building."

While in Chicago, Yandell made a seven-foot statue of Kentucky's best-known pioneer, Daniel Boone. She molded Boone wearing buckskin clothes and a coonskin hat. He had a Kentucky long rifle in his hands.

Yandell's Boone got a great deal of attention at the fair. Both adults and children liked him. A Louisville newspaper reported that Boone looked alive. "He stands there just like he did on the day he first saw the Kentucky River," it said.

In 1906 Enid Yandell's bronzed statue of Daniel Boone was placed in Cherokee Park in Louisville. Today he still guards the entry to the park. A copy of the statue stands on the campus of Eastern Kentucky University.

While in Chicago, the Kentucky sculptor met Julia Grant, the widow of President Ulysses S. Grant. Julia Grant did not approve of women sculptors. She believed that women should stay at home. They should let their husbands make the living. They should take care of husbands and children.

"And if I had no husband?" Enid Yandell asked.

"Get one," Mrs. Grant stated.

"But if every woman chose a husband the men would not go around," Enid said.

"Then let them care for brothers and fathers," the former first lady answered. "I don't approve of women who play the piano and let their children go dirty. I don't approve of women who paint and write. They should clean their houses and cook good meals. Will your stone cutting make you a better housewife?" Julia Grant asked.

"Yes," replied Yandell. "I am making muscles. Then I can beat biscuit when I keep house."

After the Chicago Exposition, Enid Yandell did many sculpture projects. One of these was a statue of the Greek goddess of wisdom, Athena. Yandell's Athena stood 25 feet tall. She sent Athena to Nashville in 1897 for the Tennessee Centennial. (This event marked Tennessee's 100th birthday.) The statue stood in the city's Centennial Park. Athena ruled over the

Centennial for six months. But she was not cast in metal, and she did not survive.

After the Tennessee Centennial, Yandell made many busts and statues. She also did a sculpture of an Indian called Chief Ninigret. Today the statue gazes across the harbor at Watch Hill, Rhode Island. She also did large fountains for the city of Providence, Rhode Island, and her hometown of Louisville.

By the turn of century Enid Yandell had become famous. Newspapers ran stories about the woman sculptor from Kentucky. They even called her "a woman pioneer in a man's world." Enid's sculpture was good and sold well. But her uncle was upset that she sold her work. He wanted her to keep it or give it away. He stated, "Enid is the first woman Yandell to earn a dollar for herself. I wish she had gotten married like other girls."

Enid did not agree with him. "I am a sculptor," she said. "I do many things for fun. I see friends and family. I like to read. I paint. But when I settle down, I always turn to clay."

World War I cut short Enid Yandell's career as a sculptor. When the war began, she was in Paris. Unable to get home, she joined the Red Cross. She gave aid to homeless children. When she returned to the United States, she kept up her Red Cross work.

In the years after World War I, Enid Yandell made

few pieces of sculpture. She began an art school in her
Massachusetts home. She took an interest in politics.
She urged her women friends to join her in voting and
to get involved in politics.

In the late 1920s Enid left the public eye. She died
in 1934 and was buried in Louisville's Cave Hill
Cemetery.

During her working years Enid Yandell molded
many pieces of sculpture. She earned praise in both
France and the United States. Her large statues are in
parks in Tennessee, Kentucky, Connecticut, and Rhode
Island. Smaller pieces can be found from Maine to
Missouri.

Wherever they are, these statues mark her talent.
She was a pioneer in a so-called man's world. Enid
Yandell proved that women can be sculptors. She
always said, "Sculpture is wonderful work for a
woman."

# Cora Wilson Stewart, 1875–1958: Moonlight School Lady

According to the United States Census of 1910, almost 15 percent of all Kentuckians over the age of 21 could not read and write. For these men and women, there was little hope of learning to read and write. Schools gave their attention to boys and girls and forgot adults. But one teacher, Cora Wilson Stewart, decided to teach reading and writing to adults at night. Her students could keep their jobs during the day and still go to school.

Cora Wilson Stewart began the Moonlight Schools in Rowan County in 1911. Soon they gained state and then national attention. In time the Moonlight Schools and their founder won world attention.

Cora Wilson was born in Powell County, Kentucky, in 1875. At the age of four, she declared her plans to become a school teacher. By age five she began holding classes in her back yard. She made her little friends call her "Miss Cora." But her father said she should be nicknamed "the General."

In 1880 the Wilsons moved to the small town of Cross Roads in Rowan County. Cora's mother taught school, and her father was a country doctor. The family also ran a general store.

Cora began going to school at Cross Roads. The school was a one-room country school. It had classes in reading, writing, and arithmetic.

Many of the Wilsons' neighbors were not interested in education. They saw no need for schooling beyond the one-room schoolhouse which went through the eighth grade. Cora's parents did not agree with their neighbors. They wanted their five children to read and study at home, too. Recalling her childhood, Cora said, "We had books at home. We read stories. There was a difference between our lives and other children's. Our parents had an education."

In 1890 the Wilsons moved to Morehead. Cora, now 15, began classes at Morehead Normal School (now Morehead State University). Normal schools taught students how to be teachers. Cora also began teaching that year, in the Morehead public schools.

From 1892 to 1899 Cora Wilson continued her own education and her teaching career. She studied at an Ohio normal school and took a business course in Lexington. She taught in the Rowan County schools, at

Morehead Normal, and at the Commercial College of Kentucky University (now Transylvania University) in Lexington. In 1899 she became the first woman teacher at the Commercial College.

At the age of 24, Cora Wilson was a very happy woman. Said to be "quite handsome," she stood five feet, five inches tall. She had dark hair and eyes. Always well-dressed, she wore beautiful dresses and shoes. Cora was very busy with her job, and she also had a very busy social life. Many young men asked her for dates, and she usually accepted.

Cora's carefree life in Lexington ended in 1900. She went home to Morehead, and she found her mother very ill. Anne Wilson died soon after her daughter's return. Now Cora knew she must help raise her four brothers and sisters. She vowed to help them finish their education. To keep this promise, she left teaching and took a job as a secretary for a lumber company.

A number of people in Rowan County believed that Cora Wilson could do something for the local schools. She should become a school official! Although women in Kentucky could not vote then, some were being elected to public office.

Democratic party leaders wanted Cora to run for county school superintendent. No woman in Rowan County had ever had the job before. In a county which usually voted Republican, Cora, a Democrat, won the election in 1901. Her most serious Republican foe was her sister's boyfriend!

Cora Wilson became a strong leader in Rowan County. She did a good job as superintendent and was well-liked by teachers and parents. She also married Alexander Stewart while she was superintendent. As a new wife she did not seek re-election in 1905. Her marriage did not work out. After the death of their son, she and her husband divorced in 1910.

In the midst of these sad problems, Cora Wilson Stewart won a second term as county school superintendent in 1909. Even with her success, Cora felt guilty about her personal life. To forget her problems, she threw herself into her work. She soon brought education reforms to Rowan County and around the state. She also became a leader in the Kentucky Education Association (KEA). The KEA chose her as its first woman president in 1911.

Living and working in the rural Kentucky hills gave Stewart a new and different view of education. She knew that rural people often had not had the chance to learn to read and write. They were not lazy or stupid. If someone would teach them, they would learn.

As school superintendent, Cora Stewart often acted as a secretary for area people who did not read. She read and wrote letters for them. But she felt that she was guilty of a "bad kindness." She said, "I ought to have been teaching them to read and write. I knew they wanted to learn. I could see it in their eyes."

In the summer of 1911, three uneducated adults told Stewart that they wanted to learn to read and write for themselves. Because working adults could not go to school during the day, Stewart decided to hold classes in the evening. Classes would meet on nights when the moon was bright so the students could see to travel. For this reason Cora Stewart called the classes the Moonlight Schools.

The Moonlight Schools began on September 5, 1911. Cora Stewart later said, "It was the brightest moonlight night the world has ever seen." She had expected 150 students. But more than 1,200 men and women came to the 50 Moonlight Schools. The youngest was 18 and the oldest was a school girl of 86!

The first session of the Moonlight Schools lasted for eight weeks. Classes met from 6:00 to 8:00 o'clock each Monday through Thursday evening. Many of the older people only wanted to learn to sign their names. But most learned to read and write.

There were no good reading books for adult new readers. Stories about kittens, dolls, and toys were insulting to adults. So Cora Stewart wrote her own reading lessons about community news. She put the news items in the newspaper called *The Moonlighter*.

The first lesson had 23 words. It read:

Can we win?
Can we win what?
Can we win the prize?
Yes, we can win.
See us try.
And see us win.

Later lessons had longer sentences. News items like "Bill Smith is building a new barn" and "John Brown has moved to Kansas" sparked interest. Readers did not want to stop. They wanted to read the next sentences to find out what other friends were doing. The *Moonlighter* let new readers be newspaper readers from the very first lesson.

After the reading and writing lessons, there were drills on other subjects. The subjects included history, English, health, geography, home economics, agriculture, and good roads. The drills were for anyone who wanted to stay and learn more. The Moonlight School students quickly showed that adults could learn to read and write.

Stewart kept students interested in the night classes by having contests for the best readers. She also gave a small Bible to every student who wrote a letter of thanks for the Moonlight Schools.

Stories about the success of the Moonlight Schools began to spread around the state. Other counties set up schools, too. Soon the Moonlight Schools were found in most parts of the state. Cora Stewart wrote an adult reading book. It was called *The Country Life Reader, First Book*. Later, came a *Second Book* and a *Third Book*.

Soon other states began to set up Moonlight Schools. They began in Tennessee, Virginia, West Virginia, North Carolina, South Carolina, Georgia, Alabama, Texas, and Oklahoma. These schools used the reading aids that Cora Wilson Stewart had first used in Rowan County.

In 1914 Stewart spoke about illiteracy to the Kentucky General Assembly. She convinced them to set up the Kentucky Illiteracy Commission (KIC). (The new commission, begun in 1985, is called the Kentucky Literacy Commission.) The KIC wanted to teach every adult Kentuckian to read and write by 1920.

Cora Wilson Stewart, the KIC's first president, did not get any pay for her work. She asked others to help her. She called upon people from all walks of life. She felt that anyone who could read could help those who did not read.

Stewart talked to the Kentucky Education Association and to many women's clubs. She wrote letters to newspapers around the state, and they ran stories about the Moonlight Schools. Stewart also set up the Woman's Forward Kentucky Movement. This group raised $8,000 in five weeks to help the Moonlight Schools.

She even asked Governor James B. McCreary to help. He thought the KIC's goal was a good one. He got the legislature to give the KIC $5,000 a year. He also asked everyone in the state to fight illiteracy. He called it "Kentucky's War on Illiteracy."

Cora Wilson Stewart's cause was aided by America's entry into World War I. In the spring of 1917 illiterate boys were swept along with others into the army. Before 1917 they had been barred from army service. Now the government stopped this ban and let them in.

Stewart told the newspapers that many Kentucky soldiers had joined the army by making an "X" on their army papers. These men would make up 15 regiments in the army. A regiment was an army group of about 2,000 men.

Stewart and the KIC knew that they had a big job to do. In July 1917, she began a summer school program. Once again she wrote a reader for her students. She called it *The Soldier's First Book*. It had lessons on war, guns, camps, flags, tents, bulletin boards, parade grounds, and army life.

Some 50,000 *Country Life Readers* were given to American soldiers in France. The lessons helped them keep up their skills as readers. The lessons also helped them keep up with things at home. When the war ended in 1918, Cora Wilson Stewart's books kept on being used.

Cora Wilson Stewart's program was a good one. At least 130,000 Kentucky men and women learned to read and write. But the government of Kentucky did not fund the Illiteracy Commission after 1920. Views on education had changed again. Education leaders favored children's schooling over adult education. They also frowned upon using non-teachers as tutors.

Kentucky did not pay much attention to Cora Wilson Stewart after 1920. But in the 1920s and the 1930s she kept on working to rid the country of illiteracy. She became well-known at the national level. She served on the board of the National Education Association. She gave speeches in Canada, Switzerland, and Scotland. She headed the illiteracy section of the World Conference on Education five times.

Stewart became known around the world as the "Moonlight School Lady." She got one vote for president of the United States at the Democratic Convention of 1920. In 1925 she won *Pictorial Review's* $5,000 prize for aiding human welfare. In 1930 she got a national award for her service to education. In Kentucky, the KEA and several women's clubs honored her as well.

In 1936 Cora Wilson Stewart retired from her war on illiteracy. She left Kentucky and settled in North Carolina and Arkansas. She died in 1958 at the age of 83 and was buried in North Carolina.

It is a shame that so few listened to Cora Wilson

Stewart in the 1920s. But her gift to Kentucky is a lasting one. Today there is a new Kentucky Literacy Commission with programs in many counties. Its students and teachers are from all walks of life. They work together to end illiteracy in Kentucky.

# Mary Breckinridge, 1881–1965: Nurse-Midwife

In the early years of the 20th century there was almost no medical care in rural America. Newborn babies and their mothers rarely got medical attention. In the Kentucky mountains women often accepted the help of dirty "granny" midwives. Sometimes they had their babies alone. Mountain mothers and babies truly needed trained medical care. A strong-willed Kentucky woman named Mary Breckinridge decided to help them.

Born in 1881, Mary Breckinridge grew up a happy-go-lucky girl with few concerns. In 1925, at the age of 44, she set up a health care program. This program was known as the Frontier Nursing Service and was usually called the FNS. As a nurse-midwife, Mary rode horseback over rough mountain trails in Eastern Kentucky. Here she delivered babies and cared for the sick in lonely cabins.

Concern for others came easily to Mary

Breckinridge. Her family had come to Kentucky after the American Revolution. They were always interested in the needs of others. Mary's grandfather was vice president of the United States. Other relatives had held important posts in government. Mary's father served as American minister to Russia in the 1890s. Her mother found homes for orphans. Several cousins were doctors, teachers, and writers. Others tried to find ways to help people help themselves.

For many years, however, Mary did not have a special cause. She lived the life of a well-to-do wife and mother. Then she suffered great personal losses. Her daughter Polly and son Breckie died, and her marriage ended in divorce. But Mary Breckinridge refused to give in to self-pity. Instead she decided to spend the rest of her life helping others. She vowed to use her nurse's training to improve the lives of other women's babies.

At the end of World War I, Breckinridge went to Europe to nurse sick children in war-torn France. There she met health workers from many countries. Some of the nurses were different from American nurses. "In France," she wrote, "midwives are not nurses. In America nurses are not midwives. But in England trained women are both nurses and midwives." She soon decided that nurse-midwifery would improve health care in rural America. (The word "midwifery" is pronounced "mid-WIFF-ery.")

Since she believed it "better to do something before talking about it," Mary Breckinridge spent the summer of 1923 in the Kentucky mountains. Wearing out 13 horses and 3 mules, she traveled some 650 miles in Leslie, Knott, and Owsley counties. There she learned about rough trails, swiftly rising creeks, and falling rocks. She also studied the area's poor health conditions.

On her travels she found 53 "granny women" who delivered, or "cotched," babies. Many of the grannies covered their hands with hog grease for the birth. None of them had nurse's training. Some of them did a good job, but others were filthy. Yet what would the area do without them? One country doctor said, "I can't go to every hoot-owl hollow. We need midwives here. I wish they might be nurses, too."

Within two years, Mary Breckinridge would make that wish come true. But first she had to become a nurse-midwife. Since no midwifery schools were in the United States, she went to England to study. She also studied the nursing program of Scotland's Highlands and Islands Medical and Nursing Service. Scotland reminded her of the Kentucky mountains. Many of the things she saw in Scotland became models for her health program.

Finally, on May 28, 1925, Mary Breckinridge called a meeting at the Capitol Hotel in Frankfort. She wanted to tell her friends and relatives about her ideas. She talked about the needs of the people in Leslie County.

She told how disease and death affected these Kentuckians. "In America the death rate for women in childbirth," she said, "is very high. Every year we lose almost 20,000 mothers. Every year nearly 200,000 babies die at birth or soon after. In fact, more mothers have died in childbirth than men in all wars we have fought."

When the meeting ended, the Kentucky Committee for Mothers and Babies had begun. (The name FNS was not used until 1928.) Mary Breckinridge was the director. They hired nurse-midwives and built clinics in the southeastern Kentucky mountains. The health care program included medical, dental, and surgical care for the whole family. If needed, the nurses would take patients to big city hospitals outside the mountains. The plans were large, but this health program was greatly needed.

Mary Breckinridge's job was not easy. Leslie County was very poor and far away from everything. There were no doctors, telephones, railroads, or electricity. There were just a few roads.

Most of the people in Leslie County lived along narrow creek banks. To reach their homes a nurse-midwife had to go on foot or by mule or horse. The poor soil of the hillsides produced few crops. Not many game animals remained in the forests. Lumber camps and coal mines hired only a handful of men and paid

low wages.  An FNS survey found that the average
family made only $87.50 a year.

In September 1925, Mary Breckinridge and two
other nurse-midwives opened the first FNS clinic in
Hyden.  By the end of the month they had seen 233
patients.  They made 164 home visits and gave 364
shots.  They delivered 4 babies and booked 20 more
mothers-to-be.

Some of the granny midwives began wild stories
that the new nurses turned baby boys into bears.  But
people soon learned that the stories were untrue.  The
nurse-midwives were to be trusted.  Mary declared,
"Baby 'cotchers' leave work to nurse-midwives!"

During the first five years the FNS grew rapidly.
Mary Breckinridge and her nurses cared for people in an
area of 448,000 acres.  To meet the need, the FNS built
a hospital at Hyden and six more clinics.  The clinics
were located at Beech Fork, Possum Bend, Red Bird,
Flat Creek, Brutus, and Bowlingtown.  The problems of
building each place came under the watchful eye of the
untiring "Mountain Mary."

Since Mary Breckinridge began the FNS with less
than $1,200, more money was always needed.  Each
year she spent 6 to 12 weeks making speeches about her
work.  She went to Louisville and Lexington to find
help.  She also went to the large cities of the East and
Midwest.  By 1931 the FNS had 15 support committees
outside the mountains.

Like many other Breckinridges, Mary had a bent for public speaking. A plain woman, she came alive when she talked about the FNS. Although she always needed money, she never just asked for it. In her talks she simply told her story about poor mothers and sick babies. "So many it fairly broke my heart," she said.

In the middle of a tale, Mary often asked, "I wonder who is taking care of Alabam Sizemore on Hurricane Creek tonight as she has her baby?" A much impressed boy later told his mother, "Mary Breckinridge said that 10,000 women had babies in the creeks of Kentucky."

During her speeches, Mary Breckinridge often showed a picture of a two-year-old girl and a napkin full of worms from the child's body. She said, "I wanted to tell every grown-up American I could reach about worms until every American child was worm free." Intestinal parasites—hookworms, roundworms, whipworms, tapeworms, and pinworms—were the curse of rural boys and girls.

Mary often saw children who had passed and vomited as many as 30 worms. Some of these parasites were a foot long. Worms could only be prevented if things were clean, which in the mountains meant clean outdoor bathrooms on every creek and up every hollow. Mary Breckinridge told a Louisville newspaper, "You'll find a sanitary privy on my heart when I die."

A plea for help and a long ride spelled action for Kentucky's nurse-midwives. They wore blue-gray riding outfits. They kept their supplies in two saddlebags. The saddlebags weighed 20 pounds each. One held midwifery supplies, and the other held nursing supplies.

Their horses were also truly important. Mary Breckinridge was very matter-of-fact about the horses. She said, "We must have more horses than nurses. The horses are not as strong as the nurses and get sick more often." A nurse-midwife recalled, "Break your leg if you must. But never, never, never let anything happen to your horse."

The FNS director always asked more and more of her staff. To those who had second thoughts, she said, "Of course, we can do it." She never doubted the skill and courage of her nurses. She wrote stories about them for the FNS *Quarterly Bulletin*. Printed four times a year, the *Bulletin* went to friends outside the mountains. The *Bulletin* also had pictures of the nurses, their work, and the mountain people.

In spite of the adventure, the 1930s were not easy years for Mary Breckinridge. On the heels of the 1929 stock market crash came the 1930 drought. Many mountain people lived on $2.50 a month from the Red Cross. The horses and cows had no food so they died.

Things got worse. In late 1931 Mary fell off her horse, Traveller, and broke her back. She could not work for over a year. After that time she wore a back brace for the rest of her life. And people who had once been rich no longer gave large sums of money to the FNS. Fewer gifts meant no money to pay the nurses, and some of the staff left.

These problems were followed by the problems of World War II. Since 1925 Mary Breckinridge had used some British nurse-midwives on her staff. But when the war came, 11 British nurses went home. Until the war was over, the FNS could not hope for more nurses from Britain. So Mary Breckinridge started a midwifery school at Hyden.

In the years after World War II, the FNS kept growing to meet the needs of the Kentucky mountains. Jeeps first joined the horses as a means of travel and then replaced them. Electricity and telephones were installed. Roads were built. Leslie County and the FNS were no longer tied to the 19th century. They became a part of the 20th century.

In 1965, after 40 years, the FNS had delivered almost 15,000 babies. The FNS death rate of 11 deaths for the first 10,000 deliveries was far better than the national rate of 36.3 out of 10,000. Only 11 mothers had died. Since 1952, in fact, no mother has died. In the same period FNS nurses treated more than 57,000 patients and gave 250,000 shots. A local poet summed up the story best when she wrote:

Sometimes I sit and wonder
What the people here would do
If there was no F.N.S.
And the nurses tried and true.

Mary Breckinridge was growing older. She walked with a cane, and her eyesight was failing. But she never stopped caring about the needs of children in the present and in the future. She could hear in her heart a voice saying, "Look to the children." She did. Deep within her always was the memory of her own children, Breckie and Polly. Their deaths set in motion her life work, which she continued for more than 40 years.

Mary Breckinridge died on May 16, 1965. She was 84 years old. She worked up until the day before she died, writing a story for the *Bulletin*.

Today she rests in the Lexington cemetery. Breckie and Polly lie beside her. But she lives on through the work of the Frontier Nursing Service. The FNS is as active as ever in the southeastern Kentucky mountains.

Mary Breckinridge's greatest gift to Kentucky was the FNS. In the mountains, mothers, babies, and the whole family needed FNS medical care. People in other areas also saw the successes of Breckinridge's ideas and copied them. Perhaps Kentucky's most famous nurse-midwife, Mary Breckinridge, said it best: "The glorious thing about the FNS is that it works."

# Alice Allison Dunnigan, 1906–1983: Newspaper Woman

In the 1930s some Kentucky women began to work outside the home. After World War II even more women moved into the work force. The 1940s saw the birth of the civil rights movement. ("Civil rights" is a term that means an equal chance in everything for all Americans. Race, religion, origin, and sex should not matter.) Some black women got jobs that had not been open to them before. Alice Allison Dunnigan was one of these women.

Alice Allison Dunnigan was born in Russellville, Kentucky, in 1906. Her father was a farmer. Her mother worked as a washwoman. Alice had problems because of her skin color. One problem was unusual. Her grandmother did not like her because she was not black enough.

As a child Alice helped her father on the farm. She learned to cook, and she often ironed for her mother.

Alice knew very early that she must get an education. If she did not, she would end up working in somebody's kitchen. There were no other jobs for uneducated black women.

Alice liked school, and she wanted to be a writer. At age 14 she had a weekly column in the *Owensboro Enterprise*. It was called "Home Town News." She also sold the paper for five cents. She kept three cents as her pay.

After high school, Alice went to Kentucky Normal and Industrial Institute (now Kentucky State University) in Frankfort. Although she wanted to write, she took a teacher training course. She began teaching at the age of 18. She taught in Todd County from 1924 to 1942. These schools were for blacks only. Blacks and whites did not go to the same schools then.

During the summers she took classes at West Kentucky Industrial College in Paducah. She kept on writing, too. She sent stories to newspapers in Hopkinsville, Paducah, and Louisville. The *Louisville Defender* printed some of her stories on the achievements of Kentucky blacks.

Alice married twice. Her first marriage ended in divorce in 1930. She married again and had a son named Bobby. Alice and her second husband often lived apart. She finally divorced him in 1952.

Life was often very hard for Alice Dunnigan and her

child. Teachers did not get paid when school was out. They had to find other jobs. Her mother looked after Bobby, and Alice had four summer jobs at the same time. She earned seven dollars a week. She cooked and cleaned for four families. Alice was always glad when school opened.

In 1935 she began working as a newspaper reporter in Louisville during the summer. She did stories on black families and interests for five newspapers. These stories were called "Scribbles from Alice's Scrapbook."

In 1942 Alice Dunnigan lost her teaching job when her school closed. She went to Washington, D.C., to find work. She held government jobs. She also worked for the Associated Negro Press. It sent stories to 112 weekly newspapers in the United States and a few in foreign countries. Alice got one-half cent a word for every story used.

When World War II ended, Alice took a full-time job with the Associated Negro Press. She soon learned that no black reporters had press passes to cover the happenings of Congress. A press pass allows reporters to attend events in areas off limits to the general public.

She applied for a press pass. She waited six months for a reply. Then she and a black male got press passes. Alice Dunnigan became the first black female to have a Capitol press pass. Soon Alice reported the news from all three branches of government. She also had to cover society, crime, and sports news.

Alice Dunnigan's job was hard. She often said that she had three marks against her. First, she was a Negro. Second, she was a woman. Third, she was from Kentucky.

She stated, "Race and sex were twin strikes against me. I'm not sure which was the hardest to break down. But I think it was sex." She added, "I hope to live to see an ordinary woman go as far as an ordinary man. A woman has to work twice as hard."

In 1948 Alice joined other reporters on the campaign trail with President Harry Truman. She said that her being in the Truman press party sent a message to the country. It said, "12 million Negro Americans are not second-class citizens. Black reporters have a right to be here."

Alice Dunnigan also worked for Harry Truman in Kentucky. On the night before the election, she gave a speech in Russellville. The next day she visited area polling places. Kentucky politicians gave her some credit for Truman's victory.

In 1961 President John Kennedy made Alice the education consultant for the Equal Employment Opportunity Committee. She traveled across the country and gave many speeches. She helped to calm troubled waters during Kentucky's civil rights demonstrations.

In 1967 she went with President Lyndon Johnson's

wife, Lady Bird, on a trip around the country. They checked on the progress of American education. For many, Alice was living proof of President Johnson's support for civil rights. From 1967 to 1971 she worked with the President's Council on Youth Opportunity.

Alice Dunnigan retired in 1971. During her career she got many rewards. She was the first black elected to the Women's National Press Club. She was also very proud of a Kentucky Colonel Award from her home state.

In 1974 Alice wrote the story of her life. She called it *A Black Woman's Experience—From Schoolhouse to White House*. She wrote another book in 1982. She called it *The Fascinating Story of Black Kentuckians*.

Alice Dunnigan died in 1983 at the age of 77. Her work had taken her from farmhouse to schoolhouse to the White House. She was a black female Kentuckian who made her mark in the newspaper world.

# Loretta Lynn, 1935– : Country Music Singer

Late 20th-century Kentucky women do not have the same problems their mothers and grandmothers did. They vote. They have rights. They can be anything they want to be. Yet women still have problems. Their troubles often include bad bosses, boyfriends, and husbands. They must deal with birth control, divorce, and drug abuse. Loretta Lynn has chosen to talk about these problems in her songs.

Loretta Webb Lynn was born on April 14, 1935, in Butcher Hollow, Johnson County, Kentucky. She was one of eight children. Her mother, Clara, named her for the movie star Loretta Young. Her father, Ted, was a coal miner. He worked on the night shift in the mines.

Like many Kentucky families during the 1930s, the Webbs were poor. Sometimes there was no work in the mines. One Christmas the family had just 36 cents to buy gifts. Loretta got some fruit and a plastic doll.

"We didn't have no money," she said, "but we had a lot of love."

All the Webbs liked to sing. (Four of the Webb children became paid singers. Beside Loretta, they are Tracey Lee, Jay Lee, and Crystal Gayle.) Clara Webb knew many folk songs. She taught them to her children. Loretta sang from the time she could talk. She did not read music, but she had a good memory.

Loretta went to a one-room school in Butcher Hollow. In 1948 the school needed repairs, and parents had a money-raising night. There were games, a beauty contest, and a pie social. At a pie social, people bid money for pies and cakes. The highest bidder got the sweet and the right to see the girl who baked it to her home. Loretta won the beauty contest, and her pie sold for five dollars. Oliver "Mooney" Lynn bought it.

Lynn got the nickname "Mooney" because he drank moonshine whiskey. Loretta called Lynn "Doolittle" or "Doo" because he was just five feet, five inches tall.

One month after the pie social, 13-year-old Loretta Webb married Mooney Lynn. He worked as a miner, but he did not like the mines. He quit, and the Lynns moved to Indiana. Loretta got a factory job that paid 90 cents an hour. In 1949 they moved to Custer, Washington, some 2,000 miles from Butcher Hollow.

In Washington, Mooney worked as a logger. Loretta worked in a drugstore. She took in washing and picked strawberries. She also looked after their four children. Loretta often sang as she worked. Mooney liked his wife's voice. He bought her a $17 guitar from Sears.

Loretta taught herself to play the guitar. She also wrote songs. She wrote them on sacks, napkins, and other pieces of paper. She could say things in her music which she found hard to say in normal talk.

She sang at a local club and on the town's radio station. Soon she began to get other singing jobs. She usually made $5 a show. With her pay she bought a new guitar, and she wrote more songs. Of her songs, Loretta liked "I'm a Honky Tonk Girl" best. This tune began her career and brought her national fame.

In 1962 the Lynn family moved to Nashville. Along the way they asked radio disc jockeys to play "I'm a Honky Tonk Girl." Mooney Lynn laughed about this trip to Tennessee. He said it was 80,000 miles long!

People liked "I'm a Honky Tonk Girl," and 50,000 records were sold. The song was one of the Top 10 Country Hits of 1962. Loretta Lynn became a weekly performer at Nashville's Grand Ole Opry. It was the best place in the country for a country music singer to be.

The 1960s and 1970s were busy years for Loretta Lynn. She went on tours and gave concerts. She made 46 single records for Decca Record Company. Of these,

39 became hits. They called her "The Decca Doll from Kentucky."

Loretta Lynn's songs dealt with the problems faced by many Americans. In "Don't Come Home a' Drinkin' with Lovin' on Your Mind," she gave her husband a warning. The song said he could not have a wife and a bottle at the same time.

In "Wings upon Your Horns," Loretta sang about a woman who gave herself to a man who then went off and left her. "Your Squaw's on the Warpath" was also aimed at men who wronged women. "One's on the Way" told about the trapped feeling women have when pregnant with number four.

In a 1975 hit, "The Pill," Loretta sang, "There's gonna be some changes made right here on Nursery Hill. You've set this chicken your last time. 'Cause now I've got the Pill." Loretta also sang about cheating husbands and wives. The songs had titles like "How Far Can We Go" and "Playing House away from Home."

Loretta Lynn's best known song is "Coal Miner's Daughter." She used the same title for her book about her life. "Coal Miner's Daughter" also became the title of a movie based on the book. Movie actress Sissy Spacek won an Oscar for her role as Loretta Lynn in the movie.

Loretta is proud of her Kentucky roots. Her story is one of poverty and promise. She tells her listeners that

61

they too can get away from their poor pasts. Because of her background, no one was surprised to find Loretta Lynn doing a benefit concert after a 1970 mine disaster in Leslie County. She raised over $90,000 for the families of the dead miners.

In 1972 Loretta Lynn was voted Entertainer of the Year by the Country Music Association. This award is the highest one given by the Country Music Association. It is equal to a movie Oscar. Loretta was the first woman to get this award. That year she also won Female Vocalist of the Year and Vocal Duo of the Year with singer Conway Twitty. In 1980 she was named Entertainer of the Decade. She has also become known as "The Queen of Country Music." In January 1989, she sang in Washington when George Bush took office as president.

Loretta Lynn is very much a woman of the times. She writes and sings about the problems of the times. These problems are not the same as women had in the past. They are part of Kentucky's present.

# About the Author

Dr. Carol Crowe-Carraco is a professor of history at Western Kentucky University, where she chairs the Women's Studies Committee. She is the author of *The Big Sandy*, several articles, and numerous publications for teachers. Crowe-Carraco serves on the boards of the Kentucky Historical Society and the Kentucky Association of Teachers of History. She often acts as an advisor for Kentucky Humanities Council projects, and she is a trustee at the University of the South.

The illustrations are courtesy of:

New York Historical Society, p. 14;
Alan Clinkenbeard, p. 23;
Margaret I. King Library, University of Kentucky,
    pp. 24 and 34;
The Filson Club, p. 29;
Library, University of Kentucky, Frontier Nursing
    Service Collection, p. 44;
Robert Dunnigan, p. 53;
Loretta Lynn, p. 58.